# CHATTERBOX

# JUNIOR

# 101 Fun and Entertaining Questions for Kids

By Shanna Beaman
Beaman Company, LLC.
The Nested Family

Created and printed in the USA

Copyright ©

Shanna Beaman

First Edition

For information or permission to reproduce sections
from this book, please contact Shanna Beaman.

*Shanna@TheNestedFamily.com*

ISBN 978-0-9839934-3-8

Published in the United States of America by
Beaman Company, LLC

# Introduction

This book was created to help parents spark conversation with their children. Conversation that will help families connect and bond for a lifetime.

Children love to answer questions about themselves and it brings forth thought, imagination, and growth of their minds, while you as the parent will enjoy learning something new about your child.

Use this book as a game, a conversation starter at dinnertime, at a family reunion, a party, or simply leave the book in a conspicuous place for spur-of-the-moment fun and conversation.

Enjoy!

4-2023

Dear Adrian,
I got this book for you because you are so smart! This will help you grow!
I love you,
Grandma Marti

# What is one important thing your mom taught you?

What is one
important thing
your dad
taught you?

What is one thing
that makes you
angry? Why does
it make you angry?

# What is your favorite game? What makes that game fun?

What is your favorite thing about your yard and what makes that your favorite part of the yard?

What is your favorite
day of the week?
What makes that
your favorite day?

| Sun | Mon | Tue | Wed | Thu | Fri | Sat |
|-----|-----|-----|-----|-----|-----|-----|
|     |     |     |     | 1   | 2   | 3   |
| 4   | 5   | 6   | 7   | 8   | 9   | 10  |
| 11  | 12  | 13  | 14  | 15  | 16  | 17  |
| 18  | 19  | 20  | 21  | 22  | 23  | 24  |
| 25  | 26  | 27  | 28  | 29  | 30  |     |

What is your
favorite thing to do
when you are alone?

Would you leave in
a UFO? What do
you think you would
see if you left?

If you could have a
magic power,
what would it be?

What is your
favorite holiday?
What makes it your
favorite holiday?

# Describe what a perfect day is to you.

What do you
like to do on
rainy days?

# What do you like to do on sunny days?

# What can you do to make someone feel special?

Would you change your bedroom if you had the choice? If so, what would you change?

What is the best
thing about friends?

# What have you done that you are proud of doing?

What animal are
you most like?
Why do you
think that?

What is the best
thing about being a
part of a family?

If someone gave you twenty dollars, what would you do with it?

If you had three
wishes from a
genie, what
would they be?

What is one thing
you would not want
to live without?

Who is your favorite
cartoon character?

Do you have a
favorite uncle?
If so, what makes
him your favorite?

Do you have a favorite Aunt? If so, what makes her your favorite?

# What makes
# you smile?

If you could choose
anything for dinner,
what would it be?

# What is your favorite thing to do with your dad?

What is your
favorite thing to
do with your mom?

# What do you like best about your grandfather?

What do you like
best about your
grandmother?

# What is your favorite thing to do at home?

If you went on a treasure hunt, what treasure would you hope to find?

What is something
that helps you fall
asleep at night?

If you were allowed
to make a huge mess,
what mess would you
make?

If you were leaving your house for one week, what three things would you take with you?

If you were in charge of creating a new holiday, what would you name it and when would it be?

What scares you?
Why is it scary?

# What is the funniest thing you can think of?

If animals could
talk, what would
they say to you?

What is your favorite sport? Why is it your favorite sport?

What are you
good at doing?

# What is the bravest thing you have ever done?

Do you
remember losing
your first tooth?
Tell me about it.

What is your
favorite thing to
do in the winter?

What does your
family do that
makes you happy?

Do you like to sleep
late in the morning?
Why or why not?

Do you want to live
to be **100** years old?
Why or why not?

What is the best
thing about having
a birthday?

HAPPY

BIRTHDAY

What is the best thing about the neighborhood where you live?

Talk about what you would do if you could do anything, anywhere in the world.

When you are sick,
what makes you
feel better?

Who would win a
battle between
Superman
and Spiderman?
Why would he win?

# What is the best thing about brothers and sisters?

If you found a message in a bottle, what would you hope it said?

# What one manner do you think is the most important? Why?

What makes
you happy?

Who is your hero?
Why are they
your hero?

# What are you thankful for?

In what ways are you
similar to your dad?

In what ways are you
similar to your mom?

# What is your favorite thing to do with your friends?

If you could walk on the moon, would you? If so, would you write a message in the sand while you were there?

If you could eat any
fruit right now,
what would it be?

What are two
things you like to
do every day?

What do you like to
do on snowy days?

# Do you like to sing? What is your favorite song?

What is your favorite
thing about mornings?

What is your favorite time of the year? Why do you enjoy that time of the year?

If you were an artist,
what would you paint?

What is your favorite store, any kind of store? What makes that store great?

Do you like to
stay up late?
Why or why not?

What is your favorite story? Tell me about it and why you like it.

# What is your favorite thing about grandparents?

Do you collect
anything?
If so, talk about
your collection(s).

What is your favorite
thing about evenings?

Is there a story
behind your name?
If so, tell me about
what you know.

What do you like best
about your bedroom?

# What ONE WORD best describes you?

What is your favorite book? Why do you enjoy that book?

What is your
favorite thing to do
for someone else?

# Why is it important to listen to people who are older than you?

What do you like
best about yourself?

If you could have
any pet, what
would it be?

What is the most
important thing you
do on a regular basis?

# What is the silliest thing you have ever done?

# What is your favorite musical instrument? Why do you enjoy that instrument?

What is your
favorite time of day?
What makes that
your favorite time?

What is something
that makes you laugh?
Why does it make you
laugh?

What makes
you sad?

If you were invisible
for a day, what
would you do?

If you were stranded
on a deserted island
alone, how would you
entertain yourself?

What is one thing
you would never sell,
for any price?

If you could make
everyone in the
world smile, how
would you do it?

# What is the best dream you have ever had?

What is your
favorite dessert?

# If you could create a new animal, what would it be?

If you could only eat food that is the same color for the rest of your life, what color would you choose?

If you were a
butterfly, how
would you describe
your house?

If your favorite color
had a smell, what
would it smell like?

# If you wrote a book, what would it be about?

The

End